OrnaMENTALs Feel Good Words

A SuziQ Creations Publication

MORE COLORING BOOKS BY SUE CHASTAIN

OrnaMENTALs Whimsical Mandalas

OrnaMENTALs Splendid Symmetry

MiniMENTALs On-the-Go Coloring Book

Available from Amazon.com.
Digital versions and single pages available from suziqcreations.com for instant download.

PRAISE FOR ORNAMENTALS

"...the designs are so well executed, the lines are clean and the variety is great! From cute, whimsical images like the frog, to mandalas, to patterns, to flowers, I never know what's going to be next!" – Ali

"Finding your site has brought such a HUGE smile to my face. Your designs are absolutely awesome. Your creativity has inspired me to try new things." – Crie

"I absolutely LOVE the MiniMENTALs book! I take it everywhere with me!" – Jessica

"A little-sized book with a lot of big things going for it!" - John

"Working in a noisy sometimes hectic environment can leave you stressed. These coloring pages can be a great, quiet, time relaxer. There is a nice collection of art to color in this book from simple to more complex, limited only by your imagination" - David

"Beautiful book, full of amazing designs. I can't believe how intricate each page is, and how fun to color. Adults need something like this to relax, de-stress, and rewire their brains." - Mae

"The designs are adorable and easy to color. It is a great way to relax and de-stress from a tough day." - Lisa

"The lines are neat and crisp, the ideas are fresh and the designs come out beautiful and unique in many medias." - Lora

"...everything is so cute... there is something in here for everybody..." - Stephanie

OrnaMENTALS™
COLORING FUN FOR ALL AGES

Feel Good Words

30 Positive and Uplifting Feel Good Words to Color and Bring Cheer

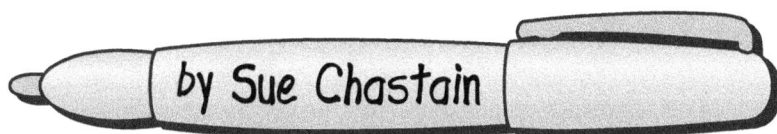

by Sue Chastain

ORNAMENTALS™ FEEL GOOD WORDS COLORING BOOK
Copyright © 2016 by Sue Chastain. All rights reserved.
SuziQCreations.com

Cover and Book Design by Sue Chastain

ISBN-13: 978-0-692-72220-6
ISBN-10: 0692722203

THIS BOOK BELONGS TO:

A NOTE FROM THE ARTIST...

Thank you so much for choosing this book! This fourth book of the OrnaMENTALs™ series contains 30 illustrations with positive, uplifting words and phrases to color and bring cheer.

During last year's holiday season, the coloring book trend exploded with a sub-genre of adult coloring books celebrating "sweary words" and adult content. Because coloring is thought to be a therapeutic and meditative activity, I just could not support the curse word coloring books. So my idea was to create a sort of antidote to the "sweary words" coloring book trend–and this is it: *OrnaMENTALs Feel Good Words*!

30 happy words and phrases are combined with whimsical and fun illustrations for coloring anytime you need a pick-me-up. When you've had enough of the negativity and unpleasantness, my hope is that you will reach for this book, focus your mind on the positive, start coloring, and bring a bit of brightness into your world.

During the four months I spent creating this book, I met some wonderful and talented people and learned more about how people were using my designs from previous books. I was tickled to learn that some people were using the smaller designs from *MiniMENTALs On-the-Go Coloring Book* to create greeting cards. It occurred to me that many of the designs I created for this book would be ideal for greeting cards, so I decided to provide each illustration in two sizes--full-page and greeting card size. The smaller versions can be cut out from the book and are sized to fit on a five-by-seven-inch greeting card.

The illustrations in this book can be colored with colored pencils, markers, or gel pens. Images are printed on only one side of the paper to mitigate bleed-through, but if you use markers or pens, I suggest putting a blank sheet of paper behind the design you are coloring. You will find several pages in the back of the book which you can tear out to use for this purpose. If you wish to use very wet media such as watercolors, you'll want to copy the pages onto a heavier paper such as card stock. Making copies for personal use to color multiple times is permitted.

These pages are not meant to be kept in a book! Nothing would delight me more than to learn that these pages have been used to spread happiness and cheer.

At the back of the book you will find some color test sheets and bonus pages (samples from my other books), plus useful links. Be sure to visit the website and sign up for my value-packed newsletter, *Sue's News*!

Have fun and stay in touch!

Happy Coloring,

Sue Chastain
suziqcreations.com

PS: If you enjoy this book, please review it on Amazon.

UNITY

ROOTED IN LOVE

Freedom

Simple Pleasures

REDEEMED

Full-Page Illustrations

Colored by: _____

Colored by: _____

Colored by: _____

Colored by: _____

Colored by: _____

Colored by: _____

OrnaMENTALs™ Design #0105 "Power"

POWER

Colored by: _____

SOAR

Colored by: _____

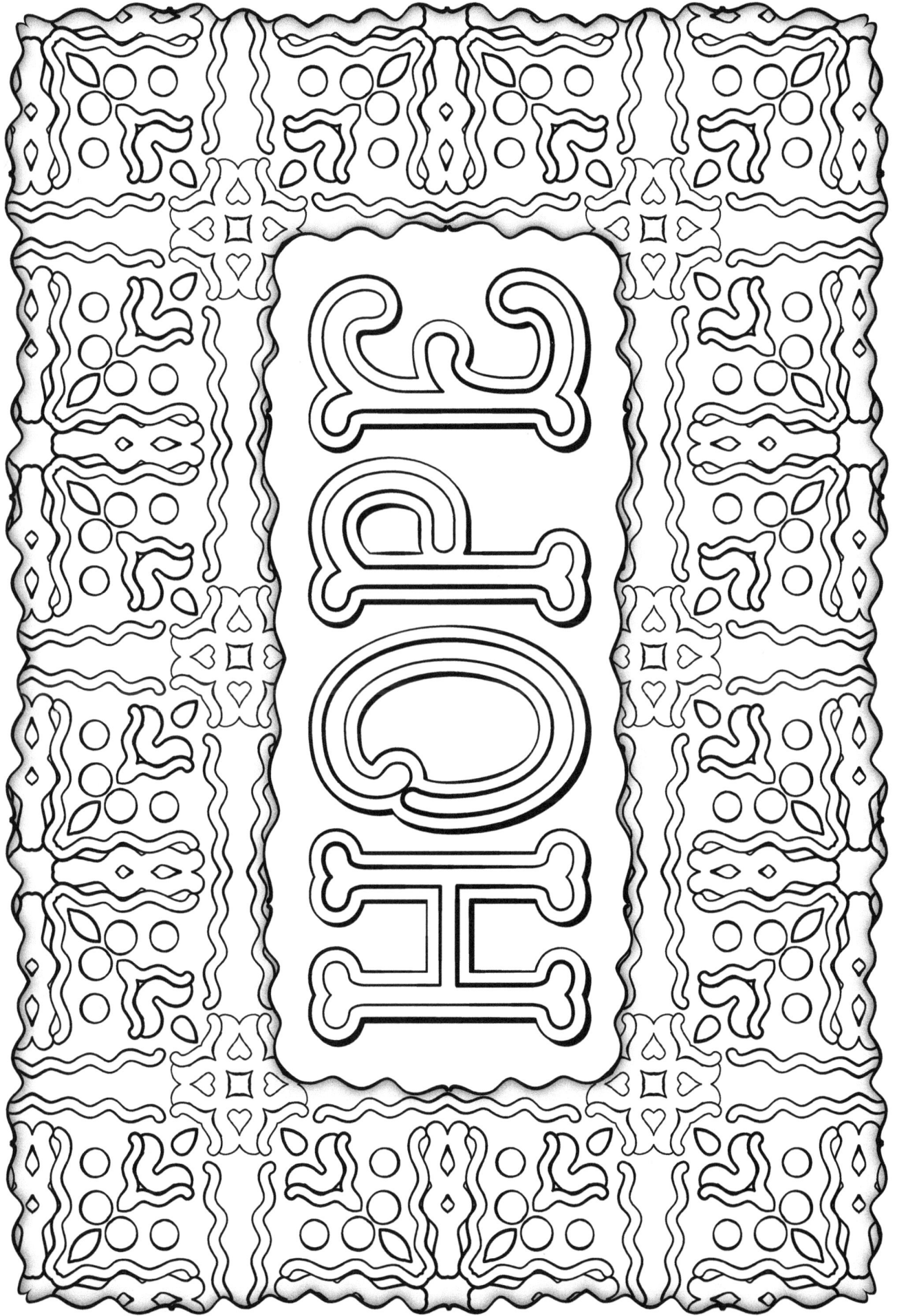

Colored by: _____

HOPE

Colored by: _____

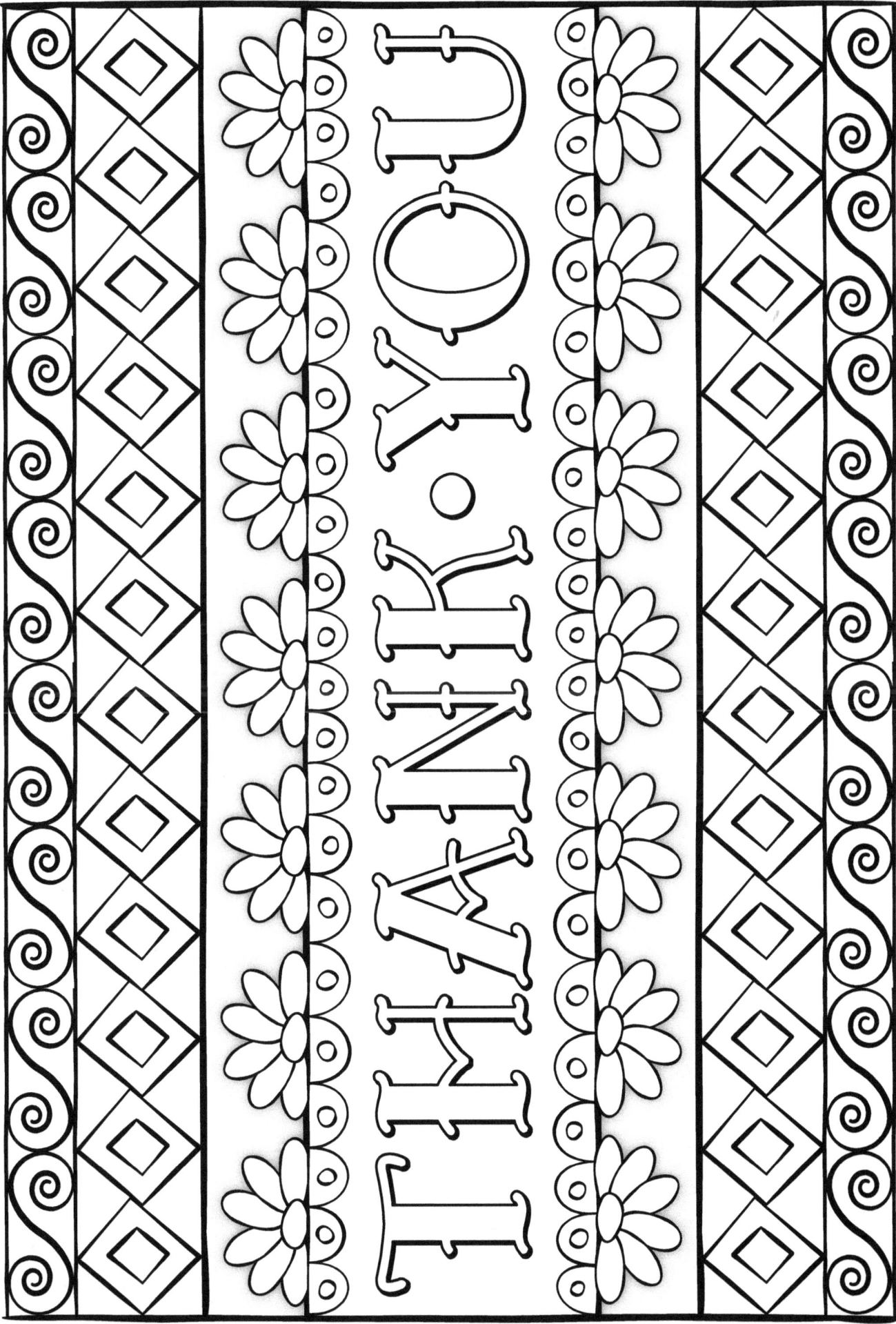

THANK · YOU

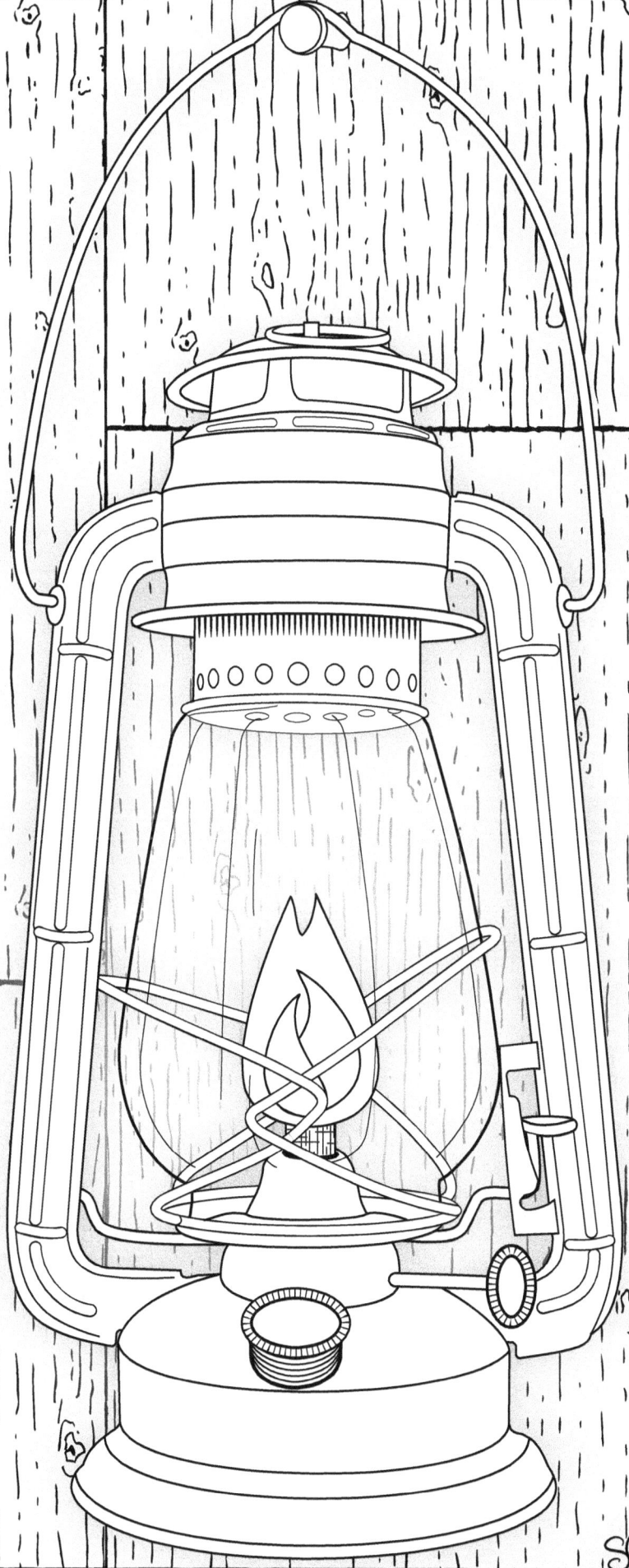

Colored by: _____

SHINE

EXPLORE

DISCOVER

Colored by: _____

Colored by: _____

OrnaMENTALs™ Design #0122 "Follow Your Bliss"

Colored by: _____

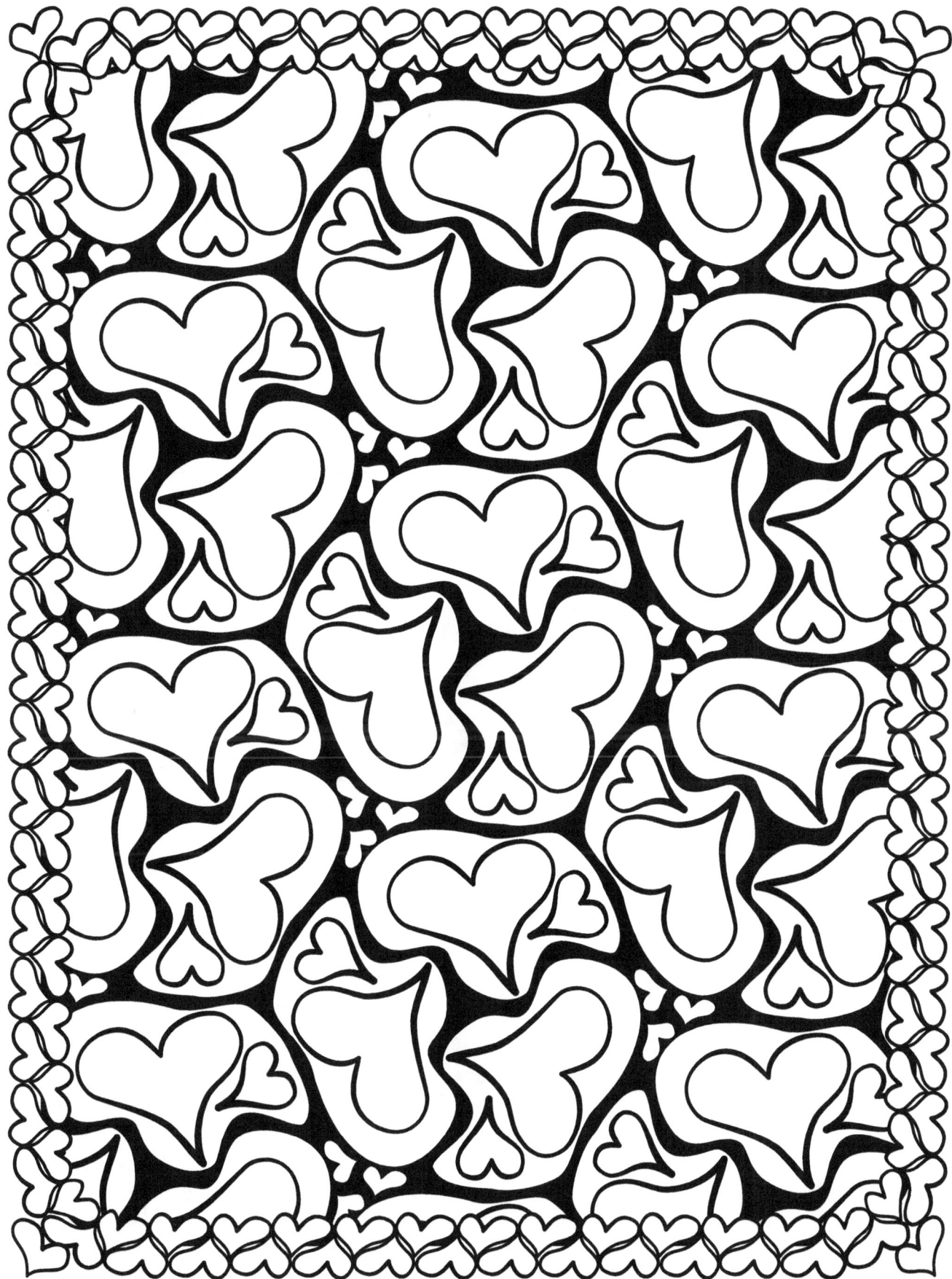

Heart Throb

Rise &

Shine

Colored by: _____

Colored by:

Fun in the Sun

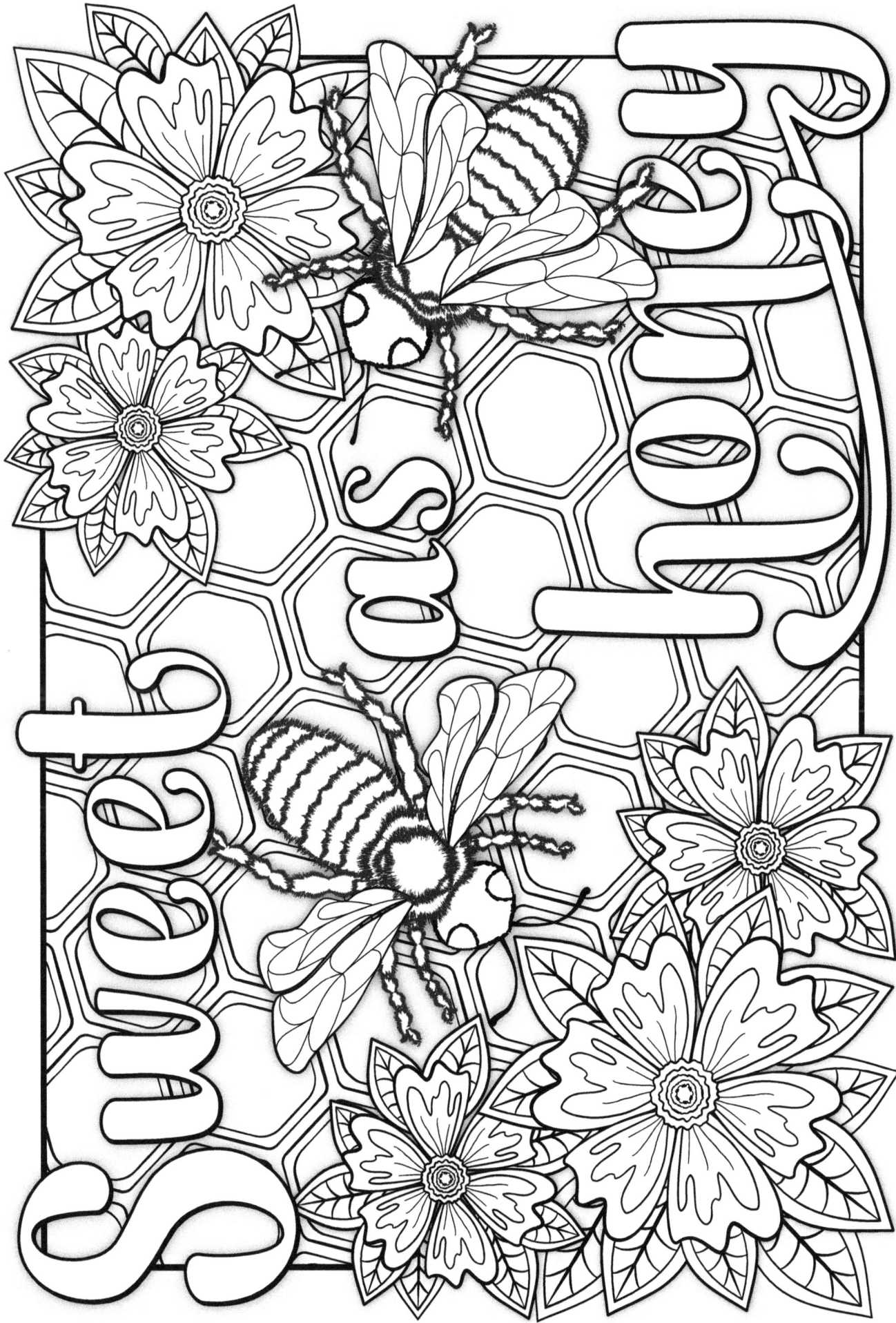

Colored by: _____

Sweet as Honey

STRENGTH

Colored by: _____

Breathe

Colored by: _____

Catch a ladybug and make a wish...

When will my true love find me?

Colored by: _____

Celebration!

Colored by: _____

UNITY

ROOTED

IN LOVE

Colored by: _____

Freedom

trust

buds

care

aid

hug

sled

friend

fun

leap

true

help

team

OrnaMENTALs™ Design #0135 "Simple Pleasures"

Colored by: _____

Simple Pleasures

REDEEMED

Greeting
Card Size

EXPLORE

DISCOVER

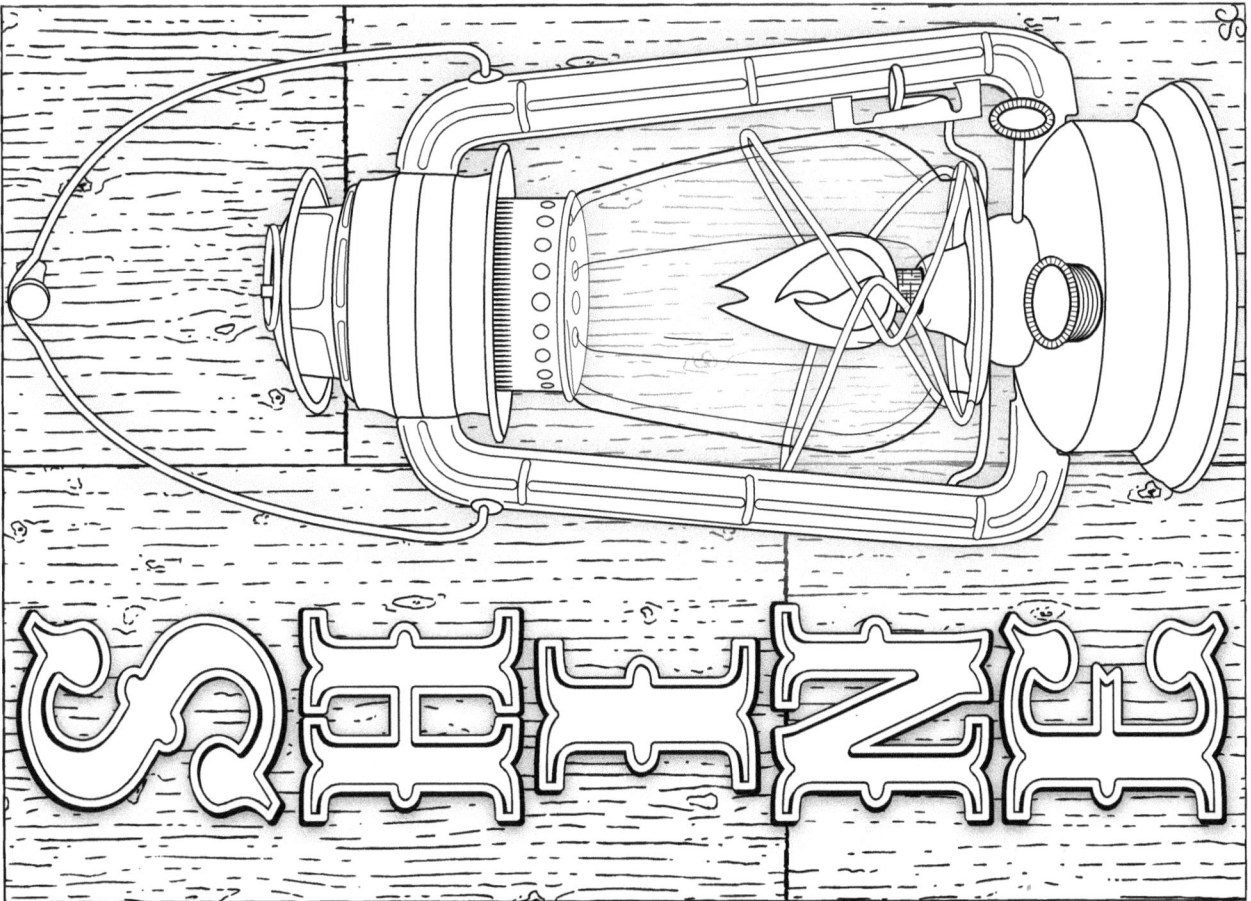

SHINE

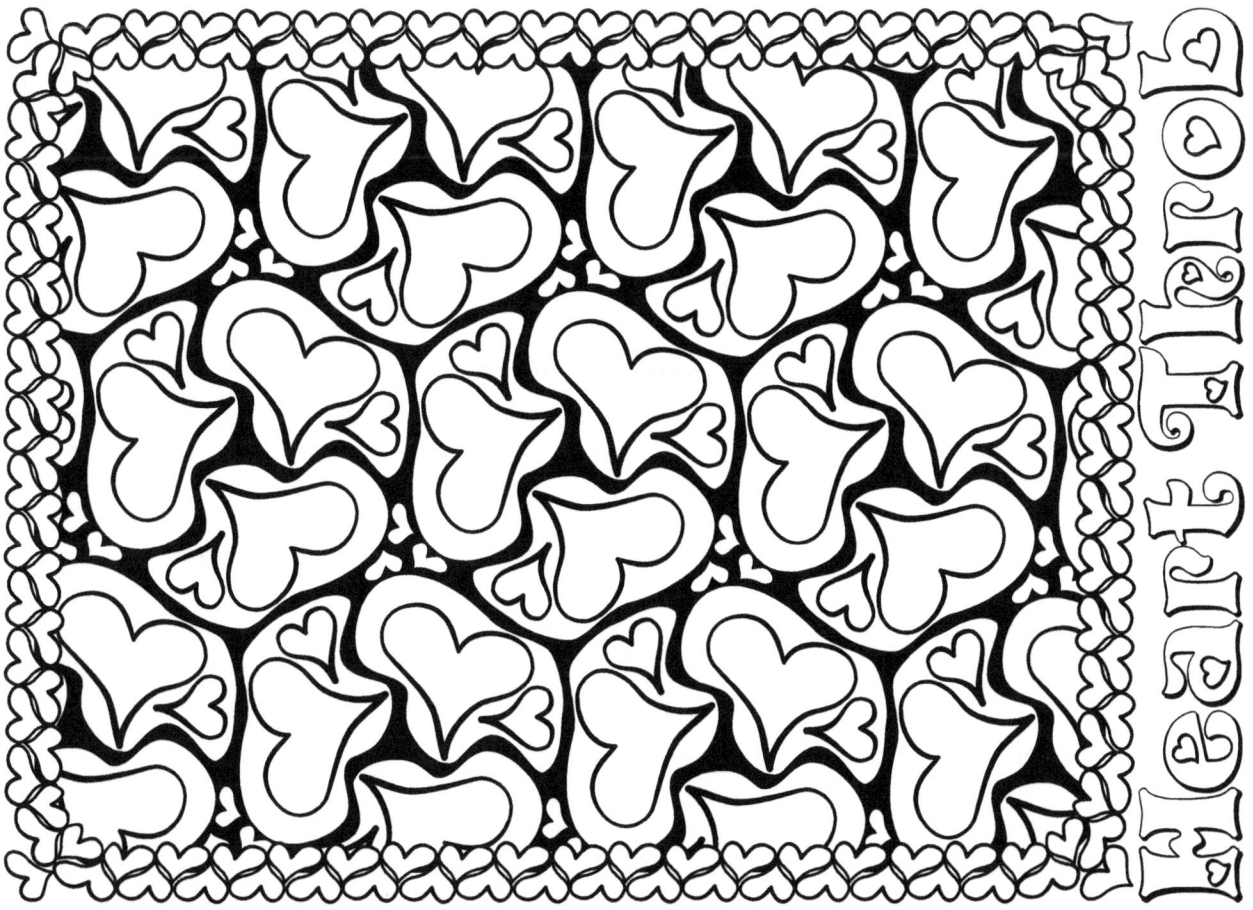

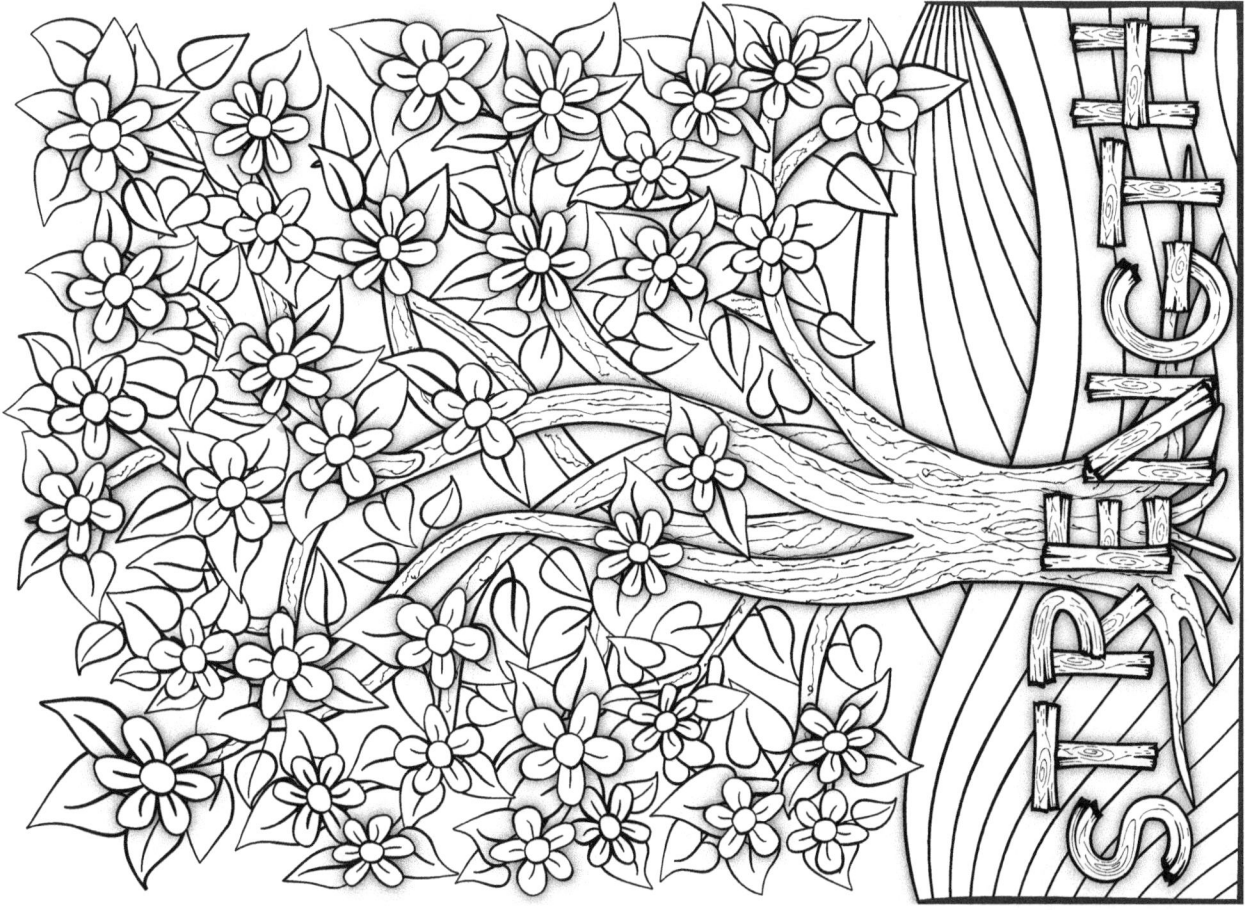

Catch a ladybug and make a wish...

When will my true love find me?

Celebration!

LIVE

ROOTED IN LOVE

Simple Pleasures

REDEEMED

BONUS
ILLUSTRATIONS

OrnaMENTALs Design #0087 "Sharing a Cuppa"
Sample from *MiniMENTALs On-the-Go Coloring Book*

© Sue Chastain, suziqcreations.com

COLOR REFERENCE FOR: _____

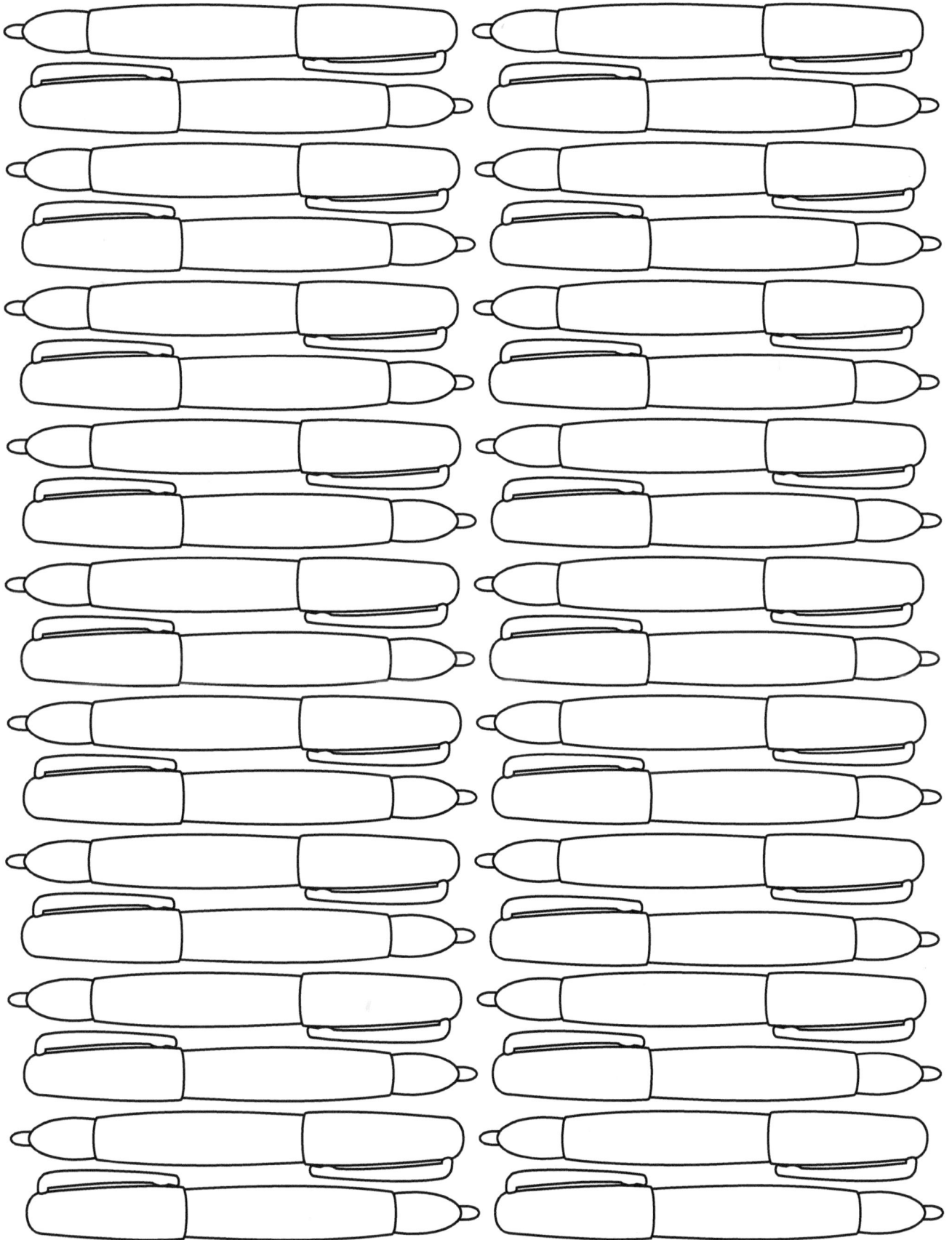

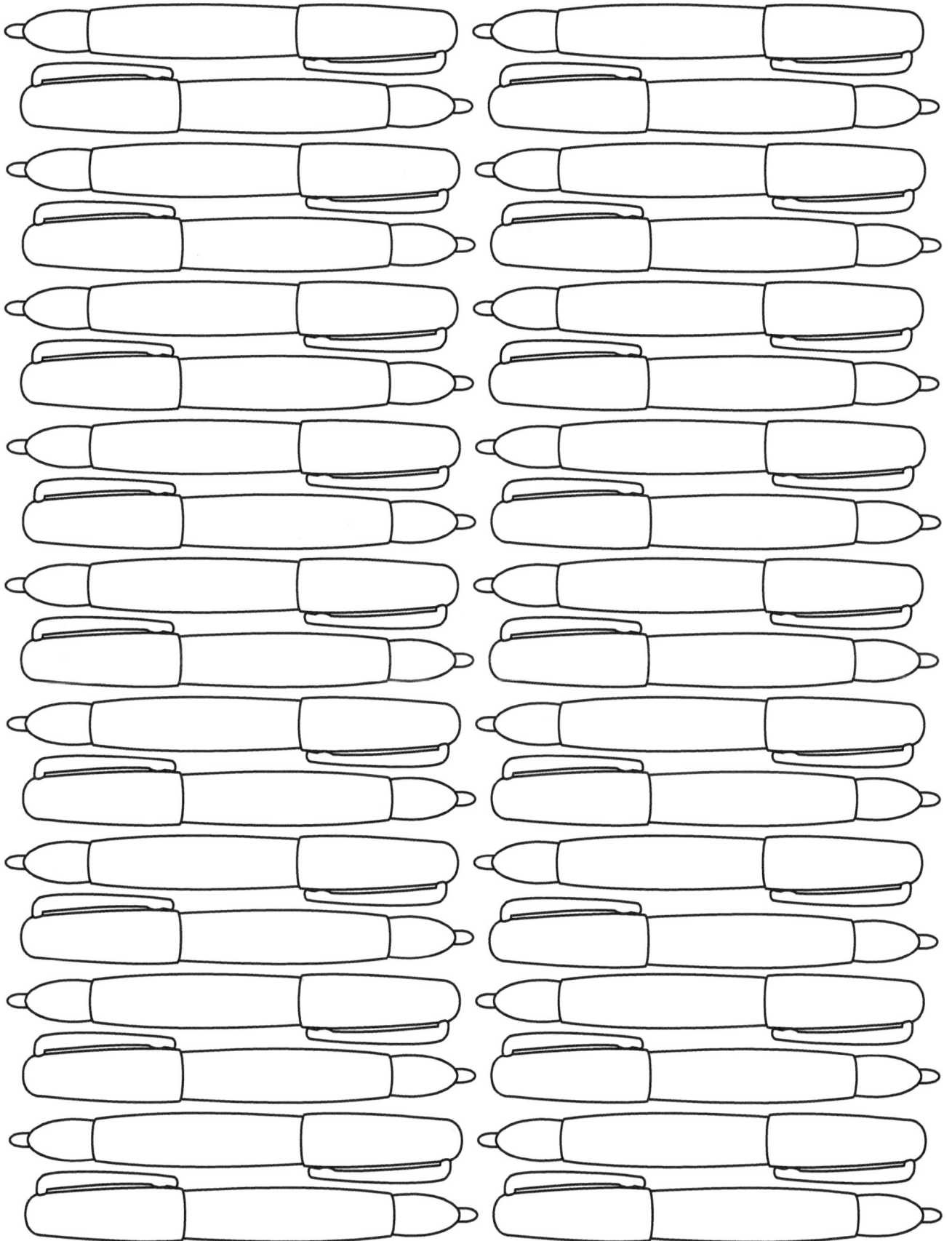

COLOR REFERENCE FOR: _____

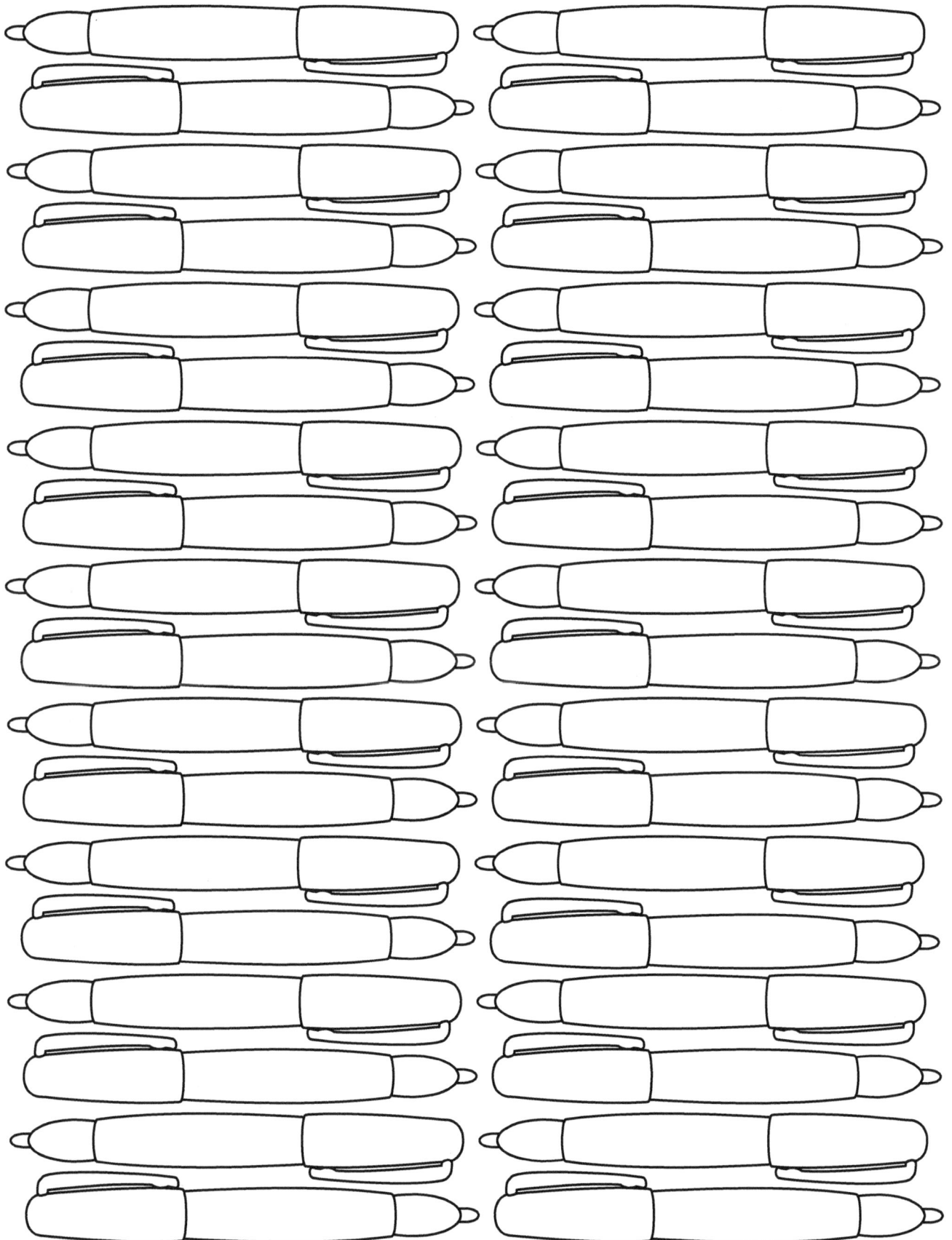

Stay in Touch and Explore More!

I would love to see your talent! Visit suziqcreations.com to show off your coloring. Use the search box to find the book title, then use the comment form to add a picture and a note.

OrnaMENTALs™ Hub on SuziQ Creations (Tips, Samples, and More)
- ❁ suziqcreations.com/ornamentals/

Color Schemes for Coloring Inspiration
- ❁ suziqcreations.com/colors/

Coloring Craft Ideas, Tutorials, and Tips
- ❁ suziqcreations.com/tutorials/

Please contact me for custom designs and special requests.
- ❁ suziqcreations.com/contact/

Coloring Books and Digital Downloads

OrnaMENTALs™ Feel Good Words
- ❁ suziqcreations.com/feelgood/

MiniMENTALs™ On-the-Go Coloring Book
- ❁ suziqcreations.com/mini/

OrnaMENTALs™ Splendid Symmetry
- ❁ suziqcreations.com/splendid/

OrnaMENTALs™ Whimsical Mandalas
- ❁ suziqcreations.com/whimsical/

Follow SuziQ Creations:
- ❁ **Sue's News:** suziqcreations.com/signup
- ❁ **Facebook:** facebook.com/suziqcreationsdotcom
- ❁ **Pinterest:** pinterest.com/mesue1/
- ❁ **Twitter:** @suechastain
- ❁ **Instagram:** @suechastain
- ❁ **Google Plus:** +SueChastain
- ❁ **Tumblr:** suechastain.tumblr.com

Add a Review on Amazon:
- ❁ suziqcreations.com/fgr

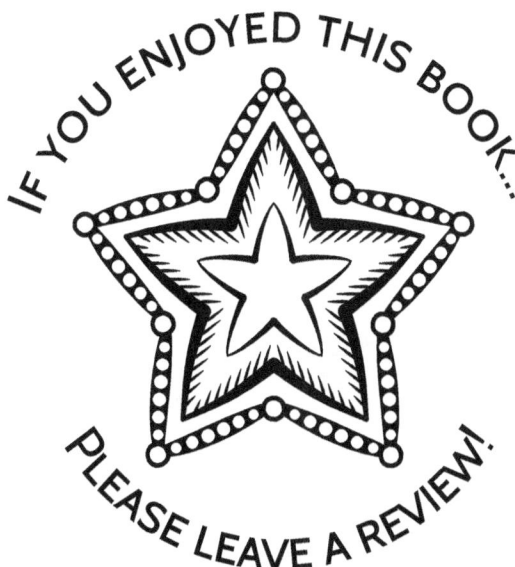

IF YOU ENJOYED THIS BOOK... PLEASE LEAVE A REVIEW!

www.ingramcontent.com/pod-product-compliance
Lightning Source LLC
Chambersburg PA
CBHW081213020426
42331CB00012B/3021